COWBOY
ALPHABET

COWBOY ALPHABET

Written and Illustrated by James Rice

PELICAN PUBLISHING COMPANY
Gretna 1992

First published by Shoal Creek Publishers, Inc. 1977
Revised edition published by Pelican Publishing Company,
    Inc. 1990

Manufactured in Hong Kong

Published by Pelican Publishing Company, Inc.
1101 Monroe Street, Gretna, Louisiana 70053

Pelican edition
First printing, January 1990
Second printing, September 1992

Library of Congress Cataloging-in-Publication Data

Rice, James, 1934-
    Cowboy alphabet.
    Rev. ed. of: Cowboy alphabet for grown ups and
young'uns too. 1st ed. © 1977.
    Summary: Various aspects of western ranch life
introduce the letters of the alphabet.
    1. Alphabet.   2. Cowboys.   3. Ranch life.
[1. Alphabet.   2. Ranch life]   I. Rice, James,
1934-   Cowboy alphabet for grown ups and young'uns
too.
PE1155.R48   1989   421'.1   [E]   88-33087
ISBN 0-88289-726-8

A is for armadillo, a harmless throwback that wears a coat of armor, and next to impossible for a kid to pull out of a hole by the tail.

A is for arroyo. It could be a creek or even a small river but whichever, if it's in the West, it's probably dry.

B b

is for bronc. He'll shake the kinks out of your spine, especially on a cold winter morning.

B is for barbed wire that's crippled up many a good horse and a few head of spirited stock.

B is for bog when there ain't enough water on top but there's plenty of mud underneath.

B is for bulldog, a hard way to bring down a steer. To do it right, it takes a tough man who ain't afraid of nothing.

B is for brahman and a cowboy has to be plumb without fear, drunk, or loco to climb on one's back.

B is for brand, the mark of the ranch. If it's too little it won't show up, but if it's too big the poor maverick is barbecued.

B is for bandana to wipe the sweat out of your eyes or keep the dust out of your throat or use for a washcloth, if you ever find enough water to wash with.

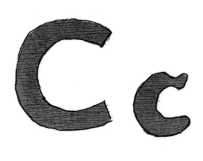

C c

C is for cinch that if you don't tighten right you might find yourself riding hanging from the belly of your horse wrong side up.

C is for chute to hold a big critter in a small space while some crazy fool climbs on his back and takes a chance on getting hisself kilt.

C is for calf rope, what you tie a calf's legs up with or what you holler when you've had enough.

C is for cowboy, who works the longest doing the hardest work for the shortest pay in the world because that's what he does and he wouldn't do nothing else for a living even if he could.

C is for chuck wagon and it don't take much arm twistin' to get a hungry cowboy to head in that direction come mealtime.

C is for chaps that keep the legs from getting too skint up in the chaparral.

D d is for daylight, time to have all the chores did, breakfast finished, and be ready to start the day's work.

D is for drag, just about the worst place in the world to be during a trail drive unless you like to eat dirt.

D is for dogie, them four-legged bellowing hunks of stubbornness that always seem to want to go the other direction from where it is you're trying to drive 'em.

E e is for ewe, a stinking, bleating ball of wool that chews the grass too short for cattle.

E is for evening time, pert near the best time of day. There ain't but a few more hours of work left and the heat has usually broke some near sundown.

F f is for fence that's always getting broke and needing fixing or getting in the way when you're going from one place to another.

F is for fiddle that sets the foot a'stomping and the hands a'clapping.

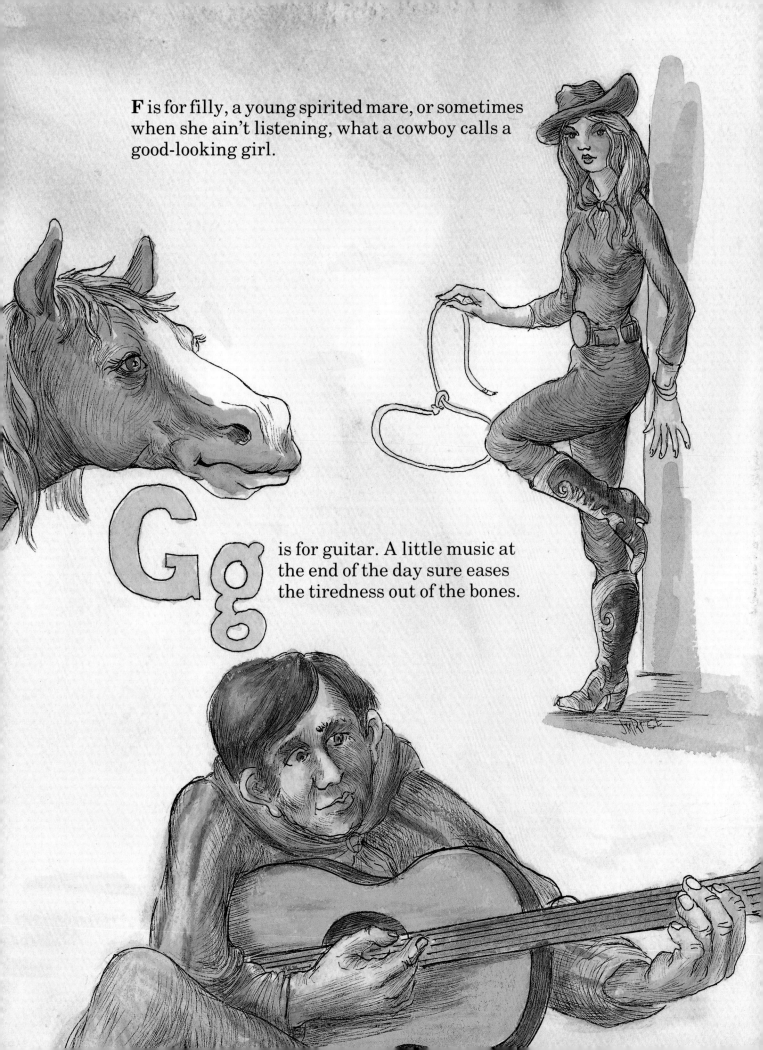

F is for filly, a young spirited mare, or sometimes when she ain't listening, what a cowboy calls a good-looking girl.

Gg is for guitar. A little music at the end of the day sure eases the tiredness out of the bones.

G is for greenhorn. He wants to be a cowboy but he just ain't got the knowhow yet. He'll hurt hisself and you too trying to show you he can do what he can't.

Hh
is for heifer, a female critter somewhere between being a calf and a cow.

H is for horned toad, a fat little lizard with spikes. About the only thing he's really dangerous to is ants, but don't let him spit in your eye.

I i is for iron to put a mark on
what's yours before somebody
else does.

J j is for jerky. It's beef, dry, hard, and tough
but fair eatin' when a body's backbone
starts showing from the front and
it ain't half-bad when it's
cooked up with beans
or white gravy.

J is for javelina, the nearest thing
to pure meanness ever wrapped
up in hide and hair with a razor
blade for a backbone. Don't corner
one unless you're well heeled.

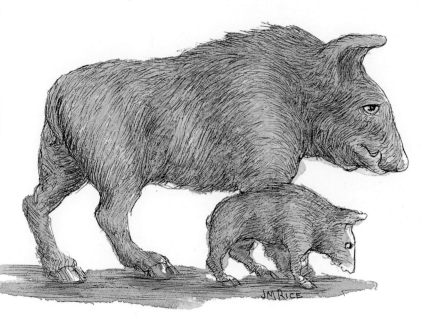

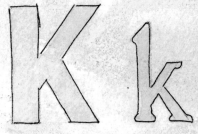

K k is for kangaroo court out where justice is sometimes quicker than the law.

L l

is for longhorn, the toughest, orneriest stock on four legs.

L is for lariat that a good cowboy can loop over the wildest maverick from horseback with both going at breakneck speed.

M m

M is for mustang, running wild and free 'til he gets caught in some cowboy's remuda.

Nn

N is for nighthawk, who gets to bed down the herd and stand guard while everybody else sleeps. It's nice and peaceful but the next day shore drags and there ain't no trouble getting to sleep that night.

N is for norther that's likely to blow in fast and cold. There's the story of a fish that flopped out of water just as a blue norther started and he landed back on solid ice.

O is for outlaw, either a man or critter who's too shiftless or mean to do what's right so he winds up making hisself and everybody around him miserable.

O is for old-timer, a wore-out cowboy that likes to come in and swap stories and tobacco plugs on the courthouse square come Saturday.

P is for plague, when grasshoppers shade the sky. It brings a sick feeling knowing there's going to be a long hungry winter ahead.

P is for pack rat, who'll pick up anything he can carry off and you'll likely never see it again.

Q q is for quarter horse, about the fastest critter going for the first quarter-mile, and he's good around stock too.

Q is for quirt to whip the horse on a little faster, but if it's used too much the horse gets loco and worthless and won't go no way right—either fast or slow.

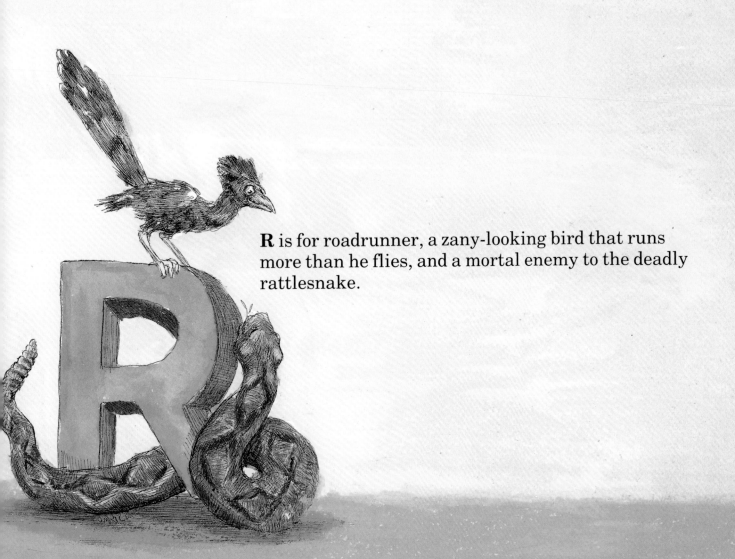

R is for roadrunner, a zany-looking bird that runs more than he flies, and a mortal enemy to the deadly rattlesnake.

R is for ramrod, who bosses the whole shebang—the toughest, smartest, and best cowboy on the ranch.

S s is for shoes, for horses, not for men.
Boots is for men.

S is for scorpion that likes to crawl
up in your boots when you take
them off at night.

S is for slicker that's supposed to keep you dry but funnels the water in spots instead of soaking you even all over.

S is for saddle, where a cowboy lives about sixteen hours a day during the busy season, which don't last but about ten or eleven months a year.

S is for spurs to urge your cayuse on a little faster.

T t

is for tussle, what cowboys sometimes gets into to let off a little steam or to settle a argument after words fail.

T is for Texas Ranger. There ain't very many but
when men are that tough you don't need many.

U u is for upwind, the direction you want to be from a cowboy after a long trail drive without many water holes.

U is for underbrush, what you'd better watch out for if you're riding hell-bent for leather without chaps.

V v

V is for valley, where the soil is blacker and the crops better. Every cowboy wants to someday settle down in one when he gets to feeling tired and sentimental after a long trail drive.

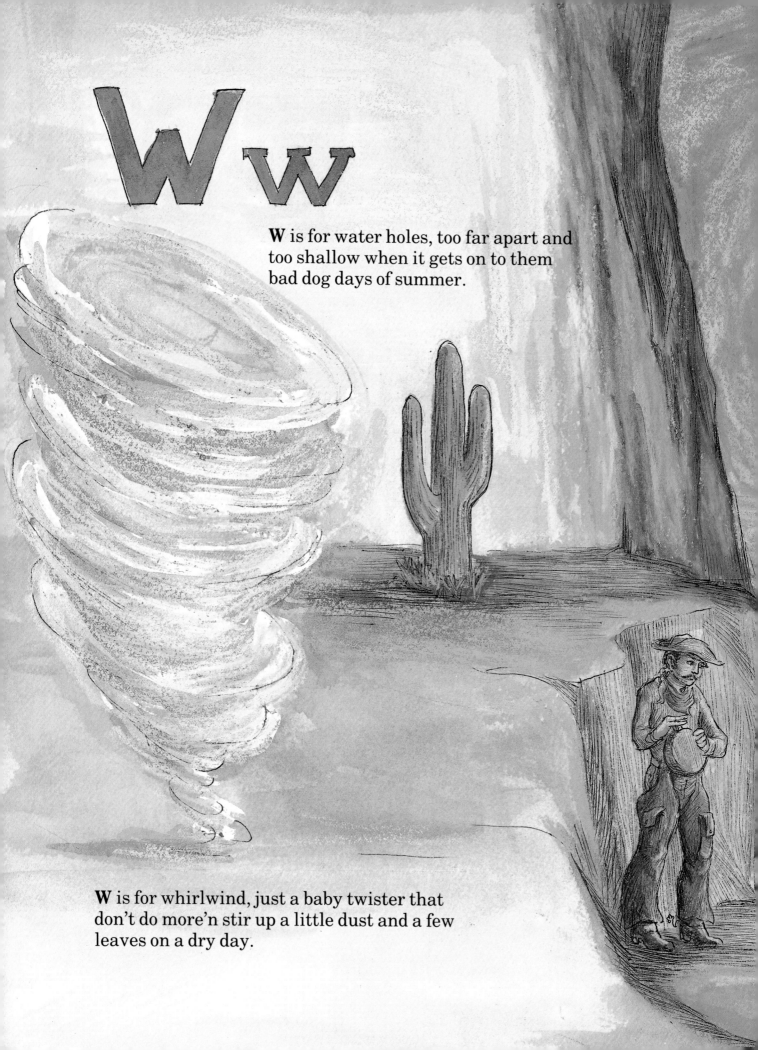

W w

W is for water holes, too far apart and too shallow when it gets on to them bad dog days of summer.

W is for whirlwind, just a baby twister that don't do more'n stir up a little dust and a few leaves on a dry day.

W is for waddy, who spends his days in the saddle and his nights on the ground—always within sight and smell of cattle 'til the drive is over, then he moves on down the road.

W is for wrangler, who takes care of the horses. He breaks 'em and feeds 'em and pens 'em and in his spare time he gets wood for the cook.

X is a cowboy's signature. If a man had any sense he wouldn't hire on as a cowboy in the first place.

Y y

is for yoke for keeping in a old cow that don't know what a fence is for.

Y is for yearling. Kind of like a teenager, it's big enough to get into all kinds of trouble but it ain't got sense enough to get out by itself.

Y is for yonder and that's a far piece down the road but not so far that you can't see to point it out.

Z is for a zillion other things about the West that won't fit into one book.